The Passover Celebration

A Haggadah for the Seder

D1378567

**Prepared by Rabbi Leon Klenicki
and Myra Cohen Klenicki**

Introduction by Gabe Huck

LITURGY
TRAINING
PUBLICATIONS

Anti-Defamation League®

Acknowledgments

The text of Psalm 114 is taken from *The Psalms: Grail Translation from the Hebrew,* © 1963, 1986, 1993, 2000 The Grail (England), GIA Publications, Inc., 7404 S. Mason Avenue, Chicago IL 60638 (U.S.A.). Reprinted with permission. All rights reserved.

Quotation from the diary of Moshe Flinker is taken from *Young Moshe's Diary,* © 1979, Jerusalem: Yad Vashem. Reprinted with permission. All rights reserved.

Hebrew text on page 21 is reprinted from *The Passover Haggadah,* © 1952, with the permission of the National Jewish Welfare Board. All rights reserved.

The cover and interior art are by Judith Joseph. The music engraving is by Philip L. Roberts. Gabe Huck edited this book with assistance from Carol Mycio. The design is by Anna Manhart and the typesetting was done by Karen Mitchell in Esprit and Vag Rounded. This book was printed by Printing Arts Chicago in Cicero, Illinois.

THE PASSOVER CELEBRATION © 1980, revised edition © 2001 Archdiocese of Chicago: Liturgy Training Publications, 1800 North Hermitage Avenue, Chicago IL 60622-1101; 1-800-933-1800; fax 1-800-933-7094; orders@ltp.org. All rights reserved.

Visit our website at www.ltp.org.

Note: A 50-minute cassette or CD, *Songs for the Seder Meal,* is also available from Liturgy Training Publications. The recording includes all of the music used in this booklet, additional background music that can be used during the seder, plus a pronunciation guide to the Hebrew words that are used often in the course of the seder. To order, call Liturgy Training Publications at 1-800-933-1800.

05 04 03 02 01   5 4 3 2 1

ISBN 1-56854-389-1

PASSR

The Passover Celebration

In the night of Passover all that happened in Egypt renews and
bestirs itself; and this itself helps to bring the ultimate redemption.
—Rabbi Moshe Chaim Luzatto (1707–1746)

There is a time when time stands still, motionless. There
is a point in religious life when time becomes eternal, beyond
recount, beyond hourly divisions. There is a moment when
we leave the present to go back in memory, feeling and prayer
to the past, to a past that is the very ground of our being.
This is when we return to the sources. This is Passover.

Passover is the oldest festival of the Hebrew liturgical
calendar. It has been observed by the Jewish people for
more than three thousand years. It occurs when spring comes
to the land of Israel, the time of renewal, in March-April,
in the Hebrew month of Nisan. The festival lasts eight days.

The holiday commemorates two events: the deliverance from Egyptian bondage (the beginning of our people's
own history) and the time of the barley season (a remembrance of the relationship of Israel with the land).

The liberation from slavery was a historical event
entailing political and spiritual dimensions of freedom.
Freedom from political oppression was not an act by itself.
Political freedom was the prelude, the preparation for a more
total form of freedom, the spiritual liberation of Israel. The
road from Egypt took the community to Mount Sinai, from
bondage to the total freedom of God's revelation. The biblical
text introduces the numinous moment of the Mount Sinai
covenant with a specific reference to the days of oppression:
"I am the Lord, your God, who brought you out of the Land
of Egypt, out of the house of bondage" (Exodus 20:2).

Freedom becomes this first commandment. It is a freedom framed by a covenantal relationship that will stress the spiritual obligations of the community and its ethical commitment. Political liberation is crowned by the inner freedom of spiritual discipline and a witnessing vocation to humanity.

The Bible names the festival Pesach, Passover, and Hag Hamatzot, the feast of unleavened bread. Exodus 12:27 refers to the Hebrew homes protected by God who "passed over" their houses at the moment of the tenth plague, the death of the firstborn. This salvation was later commemorated in the offering of the paschal lamb at the Temple. Generally, the biblical text refers to the feast itself as Pesach, Passover, since on the eve of the first day the paschal offering was sacrificed, and to the other seven days as Hag Hamatzot, the festival of the unleavened bread (see Leviticus 23:4–8).

Passover is celebrated both at the synagogue and in the home. In the synagogue, the central event is the reading of the Song of Songs, one of the five Megillot (special writings) of the Hebrew Bible. The liturgy calls for its recitation after the morning service and during the Sabbath of Passover.

Rabbinic tradition interprets the Song of Songs as a love story in which the "Beloved" is understood to be God and the "Bride" is Israel. The medieval commentators pointed out that the biblical text was an appropriate reading because it described a special relationship: God to Israel, a dialogue that became a wedded reality at Mount Sinai when God's revelation and Israel's acceptance of the Torah became a love affair for eternity.

The celebration at home is a reenactment of the exodus experience. The home is transformed into a sanctuary where rituals and observances change family life and where time, secular time (the time of everyday life experience), undergoes a transfiguration: It becomes a sacred time. It is a period suspended in eternity, rooted in the passage from slavery to freedom. Such a time encourages us to recall other historical moments when the Jewish people were threatened and enslaved, and to pray for the freedom from oppression for all people everywhere. It is a time of hope, of renewed Jewish hope in the ultimate victory over evil, and the final reality of the kingdom of God.

This sense of a new time starts the day before Passover in the search for and removal of *hametz,* leavened products. During the festival, food with even a particle of *hametz* makes it forbidden for consumption. The daily bread will be matzah, a dough without yeast that the former slaves took into the desert. The matzah is a symbol of hope linking exile and bondage with redemption, Mount Sinai and the Promised Land. Special utensils replace the ordinary ones or else the ordinary undergo a thorough cleaning and purification. The house is rigorously cleaned and so prepared for the moment when all will sit at the table for the reading of the Haggadah, the ritual text that tells the Exodus epic in prayer and proclamation.

The word *seder* means "order," refering to the ritual followed during the celebration. This order entails the history of enslavement, the partaking of four cups of wine or grape juice, four questions asked by the children concerning the meaning of the night, an invitation to share the bread with the poor, the recital of psalms and folktales, the game of the *afikoman* (using a special piece of matzah) and a final recital of messianic hope in the eternal existence of Jerusalem.

The main concepts of Judaism are expounded in explanation and discussion by the family and participants:

Call and election. The *kiddush* (the blessing over the wine when partaking of the first cup) reminds everyone of God's call and the election of Israel. It also recalls the moral and ritual obligations of the covenantal relationship, the obligation to observe the Sabbath and the festivals.

Solidarity with the poor. The very beginning of the recitation of the Haggadah proclaims solidarity with the poor and hungry. The *Ha Lakhma Anya* reminds the Jewish people that they were in need in Egypt and that slavery is still a reality for many in the world. The door of the house is open to receive those in need of spiritual and material help.

God in history. God's redemption of Israel is a reminder — a prophetic reminder — of God's action and presence in history.

Our obligation to teach our heritage. The Haggadah emphasizes the teaching of the past as part of the learning process of the present. Parents are obligated to tell the story of Israel's existence, God's intervention and the fulfillment of the Promised Land. This is expounded in the answers to the four questions asked by the children participating in the ceremony, in the recounting of the story of the exodus, and in the two folktales "Who Knows One?" and "Chad Gadyah."

The actuality of oppression. The Haggadah tells us that Egyptian slavery was not a unique moment of oppression in Jewish history in Israel. The Middle Ages witnessed the persecution of entire Jewish communities because of the libel stories of ritual murder that were so often leveled against Jews at Passover. The accusation was that Jews killed Christian children for the blood of the Passover offering.

Another more diabolic form of slavery, the Holocaust, was much more cruel than Egyptian slavery. The Nazi persecution and murder of six million Jews constantly reminds us of the possibility of evil, the most pervasive form of wickedness in the history of humankind.

During the Holocaust each Passover brought hope to the Jews: as prisoners in concentration camps, living in ghettos, hiding under friendly roofs or in the forests. It brought hope to Moshe Flinker and his family. The reading of the Haggadah, when it was possible, or the uttering of prayers or the hallel psalms, was an act of courage that confronted total madness and evil with words that reminded the community that God was present, even in the midst of horror.

Passover was also a time of resistance. In the Passover of 1943 the remnant of the Jewish community in Warsaw rose against the German army and started a fight for liberty and human decency that inspired all Europe in the struggle for freedom.

Messianic hope: the cup of Elijah. According to ancient rabbinic traditions, the prophet Elijah never died. He just vanished in the heaven of heavens where he ascended in a fiery chariot. It is the belief of generations that Elijah would return to earth as a forerunner of the Messiah to establish the kingdom of God.

Exile and return. The theme of exile and return, so central and crucial in Israel from the Babylonian exile to our own days, is present in the singing of "Let My People Go" and the final messianic proclamation of Jerusalem. The seder ends with this proclamation and the hope to be "next year in Jerusalem."

Songs and the game of finding the *afikoman* bring joy to everyone. For eight days the house and the family will follow a special menu of unleavened food. The life of redemption will be a daily exercise in word and ritual, a total experience of faith. It will be a time for the inner freedom of commitment, the recovery of meaning and of purpose.

—Rabbi Leon Klenicki
    Consultant for Interfaith Affairs
    Anti-Defamation League

The Seder Table

The Preparation of a Seder: Introduction for Christians

For more than a generation now, great numbers of Christians have been learning about the Jewish festival of Passover and especially about its special ritual, the seder meal. The motivation for this has been various, but experience has led many to the same conclusions: We do not come to the seder as we do to a history lesson or to a restaging of the last supper of Jesus. We come to the seder as guests when it is celebrated by Jews. To do so is to acknowledge common biblical roots. We come also to find—in all the beauty, poetry and delight of the seder—a deep, honest and strong expression of faith.

This booklet has been prepared, with Jewish and Christian sponsorship, to help Christians know and celebrate a seder meal with Jewish friends.

Table and Story

At the heart of things, Jews and Christians find not temples and cathedrals, schools and libraries, laws and titles, but something as simple as sharing a piece of bread and as delightful as sharing a cup of wine—sharing with gestures of praise and thanks to God. This is a little scandalous, even in our own stubborn minds and hearts: that to meet God and to find ourselves, we Jews and Christians gather around a table set with bread and wine. It is ordinary, yet exuberant; it is plain, yet awe-inspiring. What gathers us here is worthy of praise and thanks beyond words.

The Passover seder happens at a table, at a festive meal. In the Hebrew Scriptures a strong image for the messianic time (the reign of God here and still to come) is such a festive assembly. Those present are, however, not necessarily the ones we expect to see; rather, there are the children and the poor, the weary and the oppressed. So at the seder there is an open door and a full cup of wine on the table for those yet to arrive. This meal is not a cozy gathering of the saved, but a troubled gathering at table with all the hungry children of the God we seek to praise.

Passover is a springtime holiday; its story is a springtime story: the hope that comes from creation, from the earth itself, that there is life made new again. Around the table from generation to generation that story, first told by sun and earth and rain and seeds, is endlessly repeated. It is told now of something long ago, a promise, an out-stretched arm to save a people: life after passing through death. But this leads to something more. It is about me! It is my story! It happened to me! The Passover ritual says as much: "You shall tell your child on that day, saying, 'This is because of what the Lord did for me when I went free from Egypt.'" This is the great "Today!" that runs through Jewish and Christian stories.

Thanks and Praise

Jews and Christians somehow shape most of their prayers into the giving of thanks: thus the "Blessed are you . . ." of Jewish prayer and the eucharist (a Greek word for thanks and praise) of Christian prayer. At the seder, the all-pervading thanks goes beyond mere words to become song (especially at moments like the "Dayenu!" acclamation), dances and gestures (the lifting of wine cups together, the passing of bread), reverent silence, simple and beautiful objects and surroundings, and hospitality that blends the formal and informal.

In the Jewish tradition a new day begins at sundown. The seder is held in the evening as the first day of Passover begins. It is primarily a ritual of the home. What is given here presumes that, but it will be useful also for larger gatherings when a great number of persons celebrate Passover together. On such occasions, the parts will have to be distributed among those in the group and the use of song becomes even more important. All the participants should have the opportunity to see and taste the various foods during the rite.

Remote Preparations

Much of the joy of the seder is in the preparation—and no one in the family should be without some part in this. Where several families are to celebrate the seder together, each family and individual can be given tasks and responsibilities. Even when the group is very large, meeting for the seder in a hall or auditorium, it is still possible to ask that everyone make some special preparation: a part of the pot luck dinner, place cards, their own seder plate.

Cleaning the house. In Jewish homes this is very much a part of the ritual since it centers on the search for all the leavened bread and other foods containing yeast, all to be banished from the home during the eight days of Passover. Special cleaning—of the home, the dishes and the participants themselves—is part of the preparation for any great festival. Somewhere in this is the spring cleaning which sees that unused goods are put into new hands. Whether the seder happens in a small dining room or a large auditorium, the place should have a once-a-year look and feeling for this night.

Making invitations and place cards. Children may help in this task of making and sending invitations, then preparing special place cards for each participant.

Learning the songs, assigning special tasks. The leader of the seder service should, well before the day of the seder, study the service and become very comfortable with its order and movement. This person then asks others to take on specific roles, making sure they have what they need to perform the role well. Among the tasks to be assigned: hospitality, filling of the wine glasses, helping with the washing of the hands, leading the singing, special speaking parts. The structure of the rite is open to spontaneous moments, but the best preparation for these is to have a leader who can guide the entire rite with confidence and good spirit. In large groups it is especially important to take time beforehand to become comfortable with the music; this time can be important in setting the right mood for the ritual.

The Table

The finest tablecloths, napkins, dishes, utensils, cups and glasses will be used for this meal. Even when the size of the group makes it necessary to use paper plates or plastic forks, these should be arranged with great care.

The wine. Each person has a wine glass for the four cups of wine that are taken as part of the seder: two before the meal is served and two after. (Usually the wine is red. Grape juice may be used for young children.) The whole cup of wine need not be drunk each time, but the cups are filled before each of the blessings, and all lift up their cups as the blessing is spoken.

The matzah. This is the unleavened bread; it can usually be purchased in the kosher section of supermarkets. Three large pieces are used within the ritual. These should be placed on top of each other on a special plate near the leader. A large napkin or other fine cloth is used to cover the matzot (plural of *matzah*) and is folded in such a way to separate one matzah from the next.

The seder plate. A large, beautiful plate is placed near the leader. It contains the parsley (or celery or other green herb) of springtime, the bitter herb (horseradish root or some other strong radish or vegetable) of slavery, and the *haroset* whose sweetness is like freedom (this is a salad that resembles the mortar which the slaves used; it is made from finely chopped apples, chopped nuts, cinnamon and wine). Also on this seder plate may be a bone (from a lamb or, if that is not possible, from a chicken) and an egg (whole and hard-boiled). These symbols are discussed in the course of the seder meal. Each person may have a small plate with some green herb, bitter herb and *haroset*.

A cup of salt water. The green herb is dipped in this during the seder.

Candles. The candles and candlesticks should be special for this festival. Two candles are called for but more may be used. They are lighted as part of the ritual.

The cup of Elijah. This is a very fine cup that is filled with wine in the course of the blessing after the meal.

An extra place setting. Sometimes an extra place is set at the table to symbolize those who are not yet free, reminding us that until all can celebrate freedom, our own freedom is incomplete.

The dinner. The dinner itself may include any festive foods (gefilte fish or chicken would be typical) along with the wine, the matzah (only unleavened bread is served) and the *haroset* and herbs.

Special Preparations

Song. When we sing we admit community, strength and sincerity to our liturgy. A variety of suggestions are made for song in this text. Some are based on hymns or tunes known by most people. Other appropriate songs may be decided on by the group. Be careful that the words are acceptable to all who celebrate Passover. You will find here the music for several traditional seder songs, located on pages 22, 25, 30, 34, 39, 43, 48, 50–51, 54 and 55, and in the Appendix on pages 56 and 57. Their tunes, even more than their words, carry a great deal of the spirit of this night's prayer.

Hebrew. A few of the most important texts of the seder are given here in Hebrew as well as in English. This is simply to encourage that the Hebrew be spoken or sung using the transliteration that is given. Transliterations of the Hebrew are also provided for some of the traditional songs. Proper pronunciation can be learned from friends, recordings of the seder liturgy, or by using the Pronunciation Guide and Glossary located on pages 58–61 of this book. Pronunciation is also provided for the Order of the Passover Seder on page 21.

In 1980, Liturgy Training Publications of the Archdiocese of Chicago participated with the Anti-Defamation League in the preparation of this booklet. Slight revisions were made in 2001. I am grateful to Rabbi Leon Klenicki for his encouragement of this project and his careful and patient labors with the original text. For this revision, I thank both Leon and his wife, Myra, for their labors.

—Gabe Huck
   Director, Liturgy Training Publications

The Seder Plate

1. Zeroah (roasted bone)
2. Karpas (green herb—parsley or celery)
3. Beytzah (whole, hard-boiled egg)
4. Haroset (mixture of chopped apples, chopped nuts, cinnamon and wine)
5. Maror (bitter herb—horseradish)

The Matzot

A special plate with three matzot is to be used in the seder. Note that the matzot are covered with a fine napkin or other cloth. By custom, this cloth is wrapped back and forth between the first and second matzot, between the second and third, then it is folded again to cover all three matzot.

14

Festival Candle Lighting

The ritual of the seder meal blends the formal and the informal. Here at the beginning, the leader may wish to make some remarks to ensure that everyone is at ease with what is to follow. Such a rite calls for the participants to enter into and to take on fully the roles that express themselves in questions, songs, gestures and the more informal and spontaneous moments that may arise.

Leader

Welcome to our Passover seder. Let us celebrate the exodus from Egypt, God's redemptive liberation of Israel from slavery and spiritual misery.

Passover starts with the lighting of two candles accompanied by a blessing. It is traditionally done by the mother of the house. To make ourselves ready, let us keep silence to receive the Passover celebration in peace and quietness.

A time of silence.

The Mother (or participant representing the mother)

As the candles are being lit:

Blessed are you, Lord our God, Ruler of the universe, who has sanctified us by your commandments and commanded us to kindle the lights of the Passover holiday.

I pray that the brightness of these lights may inspire us and bring spiritual joy and promise to all of us. Amen.

This way of praying will occur again and again in the seder: "Blessed are you, Lord our God." These are the opening words of the Hebrew benediction, a way of prayer that is the foundation of Jewish piety. The celebrants bless, praise and thank the Lord for the light, for the Passover festival itself, for each cup of wine, for the privilege of keeping the holy day. All that is done, is done in grateful, joyful praise.

Participants

Blessed are you, Lord our God,
Ruler of the universe,
who has brought us life and sustained us,
and enabled us to reach this season of joy.

The Seder Symbols

For notes on the preparation of the seder meal, including the objects described here, see "The Preparation of a Seder" beginning on page 7. If some of the objects mentioned here are not on the table, the explanations given may be omitted, or the leader may simply explain that other symbolic objects are often present. The most important symbols are the *matza,* the wine, the *maror* (bitter herb), the *karpas* (green herb) and the *haroset* (mixture of chopped apples, chopped nuts, cinnamon and wine).

Leader

Tonight we celebrate the Passover, the feast of freedom and redemption, and we read from the Haggadah. *Haggadah* is a Hebrew word meaning "story." It is a special story. It relates our history: enslavement in Egypt, freedom, the holy commitment at Mount Sinai, and the return to the Promised Land.

The Haggadah ritual is called *seder* meaning "order" in Hebrew. The various parts of the seder are symbolized on this special plate.

The leader points out the different kinds of food on the plate as they are explained. Several persons may share the various texts here assigned to the leader.

The following are part of the Passover ritual. Here is a shank bone of a lamb, called in Hebrew *zeroah.*

A Participant

What is the significance of the *zeroah?*

Several persons may share the various texts assigned to the leader.

Leader

Traditionally, the shank bone of a lamb is used as a reminder of the lamb offered on Passover at the Temple in Jerusalem two thousand years ago. It also recalls that God passed over the houses of the Hebrew people in Egypt; their homes were marked with the blood of a lamb: "Then, when your children ask you, 'What is the meaning of this rite?' you shall say: 'It is the Lord's Passover, for he passed over the houses of the Israelites in Egypt when God struck the Egyptians but spared our houses.'" (Exodus 12:26–27)

Leader

Here is an egg. In Hebrew it is called *beytzah.*

A Participant

What is the significance of *beytzah?*

Leader

The egg is a reminder of the roasted egg offered at the Temple of Jerusalem at the Passover festival.

Leader

Here are the bitter herbs. They are called in Hebrew *maror.*

A Participant

What is the significance of *maror?*

Leader

It reminds us of the bitterness and hardship of slavery.

Leader

Here is a mixture of chopped apples, nuts, cinnamon and wine. It is called in Hebrew *haroset.*

A Participant

What is the significance of *haroset?*

Leader

The *haroset* is a reminder of the mortar used by the forced Hebrew laborers in Egypt.

Leader

Here is a green herb called in Hebrew *karpas.*

A Participant

What is the significance of *karpas?*

Leader

The *karpas,* a piece of parsley or celery, is a reminder of springtime, the season of Passover. We use it as a sign of gratitude to God for the goodness of the earth, for our bread and food.

Leader

There are additional symbols of the Passover seder that we can see on the table. One of them is salt water.

A Participant

What is the significance of salt water?

Leader

It symbolizes the harshness that Israel endured in its experience of slavery. It will be used to dip the *karpas* or parsley/celery.

A Participant

What is the significance of this second dish with three matzot, or unleavened bread?

Leader

It represents, among other things, the three patriarchs, Abraham, Isaac and Jacob. I will hide a piece from the middle of the three; it will be found and eaten at the end of the seder. It is the *afikoman,* a word of Greek origin meaning a kind of dessert. It is traditional that the children or young participants will look for it before reciting the blessing at the end of the Passover dinner.

A Participant

How many cups of wine or grape juice are we to drink in the Passover seder?

Leader

Each participant is expected to partake of four cups of wine or grape juice. This requirement is based on the biblical account of Exodus outlining the four stages by which Israel was delivered from slavery: "Therefore say to the children of Israel, 'I am the Lord. I will free you from the burdens of the Egyptians and deliver you from their bondage. I will redeem you with an outstretched arm and with mighty acts of chastisement. I will take you as my people and I will be your God.'" (Exodus 6:6–7)

The wine is usually red, recalling the color of the lamb's blood that the Hebrews sprinkled on the doorposts of their homes so that their firstborn sons could be "passed over" as the angel of death took the firstborn of Egypt.

A Participant

What is the significance of that special wine cup on the table?

Leader

This special cup is called Elijah's cup. It relates to a fifth promise of deliverance: "And I will lead you to the land which I swore to give to Abraham, to Isaac and to Jacob, and I will give it to you as a possession, I the Lord." (Exodus 6:8)

Elijah's cup is a symbol of hope, of prophetic hope in the coming of the kingdom of God to our world.

Order of the Passover Seder

קַדֵּשׁ   1. Kiddush (KIH–doosh): The blessing of wine

וּרְחַץ   2. Urehatz (oo–reh–HATZ): Washing of the hands

כַּרְפַּס   3. Karpas (KAHR–pahs): Eating a green herb

יַחַץ   4. Yachatz (YAH–chatz): Breaking the middle matzah, the afikoman

מַגִּיד   5. Maggid (MAH–gid): The Passover story

רָחַץ   6. Rahatz (rah–HATZ): Washing of the hands

מוֹצִיא מַצָּה   7. Motzee-Matzah (MOH–tzee — MAH–tzah): Blessing over the matzah

מָרוֹר   8. Maror (mah–ROHR): Eating the bitter herb

כּוֹרֵךְ   9. Korekh (KOHR–ech): Eating the bitter herb and matzah together

שֻׁלְחָן עוֹרֵךְ   10. Shulhan Orekh (Shool–HAHN | ohr–ECH): The Passover meal

צָפוּן   11. Tzafun (tzah–FOHN): The afikoman

בָּרֵךְ   12. Barekh (bahr–ECH): The blessing after the Passover meal

הַלֵּל   13. Hallel (HAHL–el): Recital of the psalms

נִרְצָה   14. Neertza (NEAR–tzah): Conclusion of the seder

1. Kiddush: The Blessing of Wine

First Cup of Wine: The Cup of Blessing

The first cup of wine is filled and lifted up; the blessing is recited.

Leader

Ba - ruh a-tah a-do-nai e-lo-hei-nu me-leh ha-o-lam bo-rei— p'-ri ha-ga-fen.

This is the *kiddush,* a blessing recited over the wine before the evening meals of the Sabbath and festivals. Wine is considered a symbol of joy, according to biblical tradition. Psalm 104 speaks of wine cheering our hearts. Likewise, Psalm 80 speaks of Israel as a vine brought from Egypt and planted in the land of Israel where it grew, took roots and prospered.

Blessed are you, Lord our God, Ruler of the universe, creator of the fruit of the vine.

Participants

Blessed are you, Lord our God,
Ruler of the universe,
who has chosen us among all peoples
and sanctified us with your commandments.

With an everlasting love
you have given us holidays and seasons for rejoicing,
and this day of the Feast of Matzot,
the time of our freedom,
in remembrance of Israel's going out from Egypt.

Blessed are you, Lord our God,
who sanctifies Israel and the festival seasons.

All drink the first cup of wine.

2. Urehatz: Washing of the Hands

A pitcher of water, a bowl and a towel are brought to the leader of the seder for the washing of the hands. The leader washes his or her hands, a gesture of purification that incorporates all the participants. No blessing is recited.

This is a ritual of purity that symbolically prepares the individual for entering a sacred place, for beginning a liturgy or for partaking of food.

3. Karpas: Eating a Green Herb

Everyone dips the green herb into the salt water and the leader says the blessing.

Leader

Blessed are you, Lord our God, Ruler of the universe, creator of the fruit of the earth.

4. Yachatz: Breaking the Middle Matzah, the Afikoman

The leader uncovers the matzot, breaks the middle of the three matzot, leaving one half on the plate. The other half, the afikoman, is to be hidden and will be eaten after the children have found it, at dessert time.

5. Maggid: The Passover Story

The Bread of Affliction

Maimonides, the eleventh-century Jewish theologian, notes that the ability to share one's food with the hungry differentiates rejoicing from mere gluttony. The matza (the unleavened bread) is called "Bread of Affliction" (*Ha Lakhma Anya*) because it is simple, poor food without yeast, and like the poor person's bread, difficult to digest. The *Ha Lakhma Anya* is a symbol of poverty and a call to be aware of the misery of the hungry in this community and in the world. The *Ha Lakhma Anya* is a promise to share the sorrow of all peoples.

The leader lifts up the plate for all to see the matzot. The recital of the Haggadah begins with the Ha Lakhma Anya, *"The Bread of Affliction."*

Participants

Ha Lakhma Anya.
This is the bread of affliction
which Israel ate in the land of Egypt.
It is a symbol of days of slavery and pain,
endured by the Jewish people for centuries.
It is a symbol also of the slavery and pain
of so many in the world today.
It is our hope that next year we will be free,
that next year humankind will be free from all oppression.

Leader

I now ask one of the children to open the door to welcome the hungry of body and spirit.

One of the children opens the door.

Let all who hunger for bread and freedom come to partake, to celebrate, the bread and freedom of this Passover celebration.

The leader covers the matzot.

Since the Middle Ages, the youngest member of the family has asked the questions beginning *Mah Nishtana:* "Why is this night different from all other nights?" If this child is not old enough to understand the text or the answer, the question is asked by the next youngest child. The questions may also be divided up among several children. If there are no children present, an adult asks the questions.

The child's question and the parent's response mark the beginning of the narrative, the personal and family experience of slavery and redemption.

Central to the Passover experience is the need to assure spiritual and religious continuity by involving the children. Deuteronomy 32:7 commands: "Remember the days of old, consider the years of many generations; ask your father, and he will declare unto you; your elders, and they will tell you." Through questions and answers young children in the family experience and feel themselves "as having gone out of Egypt."

Rabbi Isaac Abarbanel (1437–1508) points out that in the course of one night, and especially during the children's questioning, the family and the community experience slavery, bondage and the lack of religious freedom, and also political liberation, the going out of Egypt, the Sinai covenant, the revelation and the Promised Land.

The Four Questions

The youngest person, preferably a child, asks the four questions. Different children may ask the various questions.

Participant

Ma nish-ta-na ha-lai-lah ha-zeh__ mi-kol ha-lei-lot?__

Why is this night different from all other nights?

First child or participant:

On all other nights we eat either leavened or unleavened bread. Why on this night only matzah?

Second child or participant:

On all other nights we eat herbs of any kind. Why on this night only bitter herbs?

Third child or participant:

On all other nights we do not dip herbs even once. Why on this night twice?

Fourth child or participant:

On all other nights we eat sitting or reclining. Why on this night do we recline?

The leader uncovers the matzot.

Leader

These are excellent questions. Their answers will reveal what this night is about. Indeed, this night is different from all other nights, for on this night we celebrate the going forth of Israel from slavery into freedom and redemption, from a time of hardship to a time of blessing.

Various participants may speak the following questions and responses.

Why do we eat only matzah tonight?

When Pharaoh let our ancestors go from Egypt, they were forced to flee in great haste. They had no time to bake their bread. They could not wait for the yeast to rise, so the sun beating down on the dough as they hurried along baked it into flat unleavened bread called matzah.

Why do we eat bitter herbs tonight?

Because the Bible tells us that our ancestors were slaves in the land of Egypt and their lives were made bitter by their oppressors.

Why do we dip the herbs twice tonight?

We dip the parsley/celery into salt water because it reminds us of the vegetation that comes to life in the springtime. We dip the bitter herbs into the sweet *haroset* as a sign of hope. Our ancestors were able to withstand the bitterness of slavery because it was sweetened by the hope of freedom.

Why do we recline at the table?

Because in biblical times reclining at the table was a sign of a free person as opposed to a slave. We follow the tradition by remembering that our ancestors were freed on this night.

Participants

We were slaves of Pharaoh in Egypt
and God brought our people from there
with a strong hand and a promise of redemption.
It is our duty to tell the story of the exodus
and to recall the heroism of those days
and God's assistance.
In every generation,
the story of the exodus has given to us
and to all humanity
the courage to face difficulties
and to continue with our religious commitment and faith.

Leader

It is the obligation of parents to share with their children the story of Passover so that they in turn might recount it to their children.

Children are different. Their interests, convictions or even indifference are portrayed in the questions concerning Passover. Rabbinic sages say that there are four kinds of children, and each one deserves a different answer in the seder celebration.

The "Four Children" described here refer to the four stages of growth of any one person's life.

The child "who does not know how to ask" alludes to the infant who must be guided and shown the way.

The "simple" child refers to the young, innocent school child who asks simple questions. These should be responded to on the level of the child's understanding.

The "rebellious" child could be the irreverent teenager who rebels against family, tradition and authority. Here one must speak frankly and firmly about the importance of commitment and loyalty.

The "wise" child is the young adult approaching maturity, with a growing sense of responsibility, who asks pertinent questions. The answers given should be reflective and learned.
(From an oral interpretation by Joel A. Bernards)

A Participant

The wise child is eager to celebrate each holiday and continue the traditions of centuries. He or she will ask: "What is the meaning of the general rules which God commanded *us* concerning the Passover?"

You must tell this child the meaning of Passover—the thirst for freedom of the people of Israel—and the spiritual liberation that God brought to the Jewish people.

A Participant

The rebellious child does not participate wholeheartedly in the celebration. This child generally asks mockingly: "What is the meaning of this ritual to *you?*"

Our answer should emphasize the meaning of Passover to everyone. This service represents the freedom God has given us. My freedom, your freedom, our freedom is represented by the great freedom God gave us all through the exodus.

A Participant

The simple child is innocent, naïve. He or she wants to understand the meaning of Passover, its story of freedom. The parents should explain all the details to this child and point out God's intervention in the liberation from bondage.

A Participant

There is a child who does not know how to ask. This child is shy, and keeps to himself or herself. The parents should follow the biblical recommendation with patience and tenderness: "You shall tell your child on that day: 'This is done because of that which the Eternal did for me when I came forth out of Egypt.'"

The Story of Oppression and Liberation

Leader

Blessed be God who keeps promises to Israel and fulfills them in every age. Blessed be the Holy One who has saved us from tyrants and tyrannies.

A Participant

The book of Deuteronomy states: "My father was a wandering Aramean, and he went down to Egypt, and sojourned there; he became a great and important community. The Egyptians dealt harshly with us and oppressed us, they imposed heavy labor upon us." (Deuteronomy 26:5–6)

A Participant

The Book of Exodus confirms this story. It tells us that after Joseph died a new Pharaoh arose who forgot what Joseph and his people had meant for Egypt. This Pharaoh enslaved all Israel and condemned all newborn males to death.

A Participant

A child, a descendant of Levi, was saved by Pharaoh's daughter and reared in the palace. Later in life he realized that he was a child of Israel and escaped to the desert. There at Mount Horeb, God was revealed in the burning bush. God said: "I am the God of your ancestors, the God of Abraham, the God of Isaac, the God of Jacob. I have indeed seen the misery of my people in Egypt. I have heard their outcry against their slave masters. I have taken heed of their suffering and have come down to rescue them from the power of Egypt, and to bring them out of that country into a fine, broad land; it is a land flowing with milk and honey. The outcry of the Israelites has now reached me; yes, I have seen the brutality of Egyptians toward them. Come now; I will send you to Pharaoh and you shall bring my people Israel out of Egypt." (Exodus 3:6–10)

Here the participants may sing:

"Let My People Go," a well-known African American spiritual, dates back to the mid-1800s and America's Civil War. Like other spirituals or folk songs, its specific origin is unknown, since it was passed on through oral tradition.

In 1925, the great African American poet and author James Weldon Johnson wrote: "It is not possible to estimate the sustaining influence that the story of the trials and tribulations of the Jews as related in the Old Testament exerted upon the Negro. This story at once caught and fired the imaginations of the Negro bards, and they sang, sang their hungry listeners into a firm faith that as God saved Daniel in the lion's den, so would God save them; as God preserved the Hebrew children in the fiery furnace, so would God preserve them; as God delivered Israel out of bondage in Egypt, so would God deliver them."

We need not always weep and mourn,
Let my people go.
And wear these slavery chains forlorn,
Let my people go!

Refrain

O let us all from bondage flee,
Let my people go.
And soon may all this world be free,
Let my people go!

Refrain

Leader

Moses pleaded with Pharaoh, who stubbornly refused to free
the Hebrew slaves. God afflicted him with ten plagues that
left Pharaoh's people and their land desolate.

Wine is poured into any empty cups.

We recall ten plagues by pouring drops of wine as we
mention each of them. We do not pour the wine with joy.
According to an ancient Jewish tradition, we express our
compassion for the suffering of the Egyptians. Although
they were enemies and tormentors, they were also children
of God and fellow human beings.

*As each plague is mentioned, the participants spill out drops of
wine onto their plates.*

Participants

In unison all recite the plagues listed on the next page.

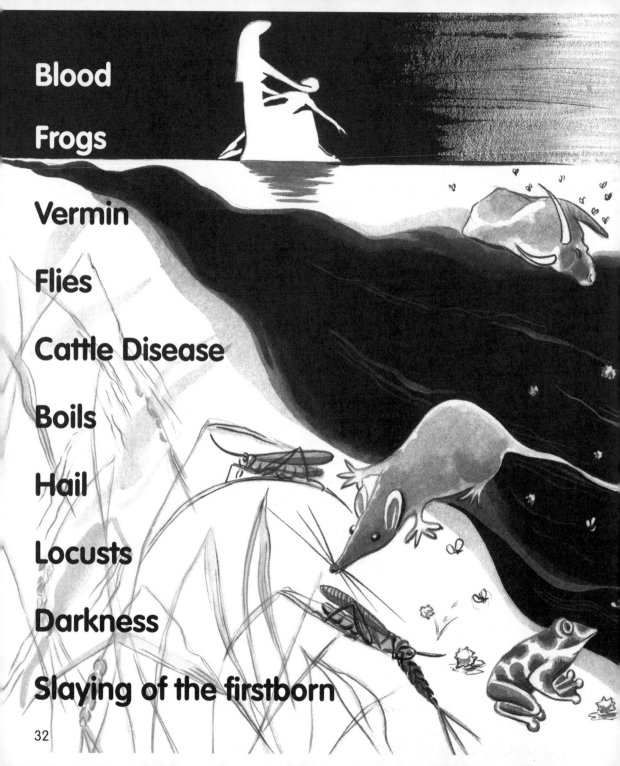

Blood

Frogs

Vermin

Flies

Cattle Disease

Boils

Hail

Locusts

Darkness

Slaying of the firstborn

32

33

The *Dayenu,* a thanksgiving song of unknown authorship (c. sixth century), enumerates divine favors and the special commitment of God to the people who have suffered slavery. The verses move from the physical liberation to the spiritual freedom and the covenant. The joyful singing of the verses becomes a vivid personal and family experience as all relive the covenantal relation between God and Israel.

Dayenu

The participants say or chant the Dayenu *refrain, "For that alone we would have been grateful," after the leader's enumeration of God's blessings. This is done with great enthusiasm. If possible, this is sung. After the singing, go to "The Passover Symbols," on page 37. If the* Dayenu *is not sung, the recited text on page 35 can be used.*

Had God fed us with the manna,
And not then ordained the Sabbath,
Fed us with the manna, well then—Dayenu!

Refrain

Had God then ordained the Sabbath,
And not brought us to Mount Sinai
Then ordained the Sabbath, well then—Dayenu!

Refrain

Had God brought us to Mount Sinai,
And not given us the Torah,
Brought us to Mount Sinai, well then—Dayenu!

Refrain

Had God given us the Torah,
And not led us into Israel,
Given us the Torah, well then—Dayenu!

Refrain

Had God led us into Israel
And not given us the prophets,
Led us into Israel, well then—Dayenu!

Refrain

If the Dayenu *is recited, the following text can be used.*

Leader

How thankful we must be to God for all the good done for us. Had God only divided the sea for us and not brought us through it dry-shod!

Participants

Dayenu! For that alone we would have been grateful!

Leader

Had God helped us forty years in the desert and not fed us with manna!

Participants

Dayenu! For that alone we would have been grateful!

Leader

Had God brought us to Mount Sinai and not given us the Torah!

Participants

Dayenu! For that alone we would have been grateful!

Leader

Had God given us the Torah and not brought us to the Land of Israel!

Participants

Dayenu! For that alone we would have been grateful!

Leader

We are grateful to the Lord, our God, for the redemption from Egyptian slavery, for the splitting of the waters of the Red Sea, for the manna that sustained us in the desert, for the Sabbath and the peace of our hearts.

Gamliel was the grandson of Hillel (see page 41) and, according to the Acts of the Apostles (22:3), was the teacher of Saul/Paul. He was a learned scholar who had great influence in shaping Jewish prayer and in many theological reforms.

The Passover Symbols

Leader

Rabbi Gamliel used to say: Everyone must consider the meaning of these three symbols:

> *Pesach,* the Passover lamb
> *Matzah,* the unleavened bread
> *Maror,* the bitter herbs

Otherwise the duty of recounting the Passover story has not been fulfilled.

A Participant

What is *pesach,* the Passover lamb?

The leader holds up the bone.

Leader

It is the symbol of passing over the houses of the Hebrew slaves in Egypt, which were marked with the blood of a lamb. As the biblical text relates: "Then, when your children ask you, 'What is the meaning of this rite?' you shall say: 'It is the Lord's Passover, for the Lord passed over the houses of the Israelites in Egypt when the Lord struck the Egyptians but spared our houses.'" (Exodus 12:26–27)

A Participant

What is matzah?

The leader holds up the matzah.

Leader

It is a reminder of the haste with which the Hebrews left Egypt. The scripture says: "The dough they had brought from Egypt they baked into unleavened cakes, because there was no leaven; for they had been driven out of Egypt and allowed no time even to get food ready for themselves." (Exodus 12:39)

A Participant

Why do we eat *maror,* bitter herbs?

The leader holds up the maror.

Leader

They are eaten as a reminder of the life of Israel in Egypt that was made bitter by their oppressors. The scripture explains: "So they treated their Israelite slaves with ruthless severity, and made life bitter for them with cruel servitude, setting them to work on clay and brick-making, and all sorts of work in the fields. In short, they made ruthless use of them as slaves in every kind of hard labor." (Exodus 1:13–14)

Second Cup of Wine: The Cup of Memory

The cups are filled for the second time.

Participants

Not only our ancestors were redeemed by God from slavery;
all of us also are now redeemed in spirit and by example.
Each of us, each generation,
is a beneficiary of God's power of salvation.
For this reason we raise our cup
and drink the wine of memory, the memory of salvation.

All hold up their cups of wine.

Leader

Ba - ruh a-tah a-do-nai   e-lo - hei - nu me-leh ha-o-lam   bo - rei__   p' - ri ha-ga - fen.

Blessed are you, Lord our God, Ruler of the universe,
creator of the fruit of the vine.

All drink the second cup of wine.

6. Rahatz: Washing of the Hands

A wet cloth and towel are brought to the leader.

Leader

We are ready to enjoy the Passover meal. Before we eat let us wash our hands and say together:

Participants

Blessed are you, Lord our God,
Ruler of the universe,
who sanctified us with your commandments
and commanded us concerning the washing of the hands.

All wash their hands.

When many are present, the leader may wash his or her hands symbolically for all the participants.

7. Motzee-Matzah: Blessing over the Matzah

Every participant takes a piece of the top matzah.

Leader

Blessed are you, Lord our God, Ruler of the universe,
who brings forth bread from the earth.

Participants

Blessed are you, Lord our God,
Ruler of the universe,
who sanctified us with your commandments
and commanded us to eat of matzah.

Each participant eats a piece of matzah.

40

8. Maror: Eating the Bitter Herb

Everyone dips the bitter herbs in haroset.

Participants

Blessed are you, Lord our God,
Ruler of the universe,
who made us holy with your commandments
and commanded us to eat of bitter herbs.

All eat the bitter herbs.

9. Korekh: Eating the Bitter Herb and Matzah Together

The bottom matzah is broken, and each participant takes two pieces with some bitter herbs in between forming the sandwich.

Hillel was a great scholar of the first century BCE. He was a commentator on the Bible and codified many rituals and customs. He is famous for his definition of Judaism and its moral message: "Do not unto others that which you would not have them do unto you."

Leader

Hillel did this in Temple days. He joined matzah and bitter herbs in order to observe the biblical command: "They shall eat the Passover offering together with matzah and maror." (Numbers 9:11)

All eat the "Hillel Sandwich."

10. Shulhan Orekh: The Passover Meal

Dinner is served.

11. Tzafun: The Afikoman

After the meal, the young participants search for the afikoman, which the leader has previously hidden. A reward is given to the young person who finds it. Songs are most appropriate at this time.

12. Barekh: The Blessing after the Passover Meal

The Bible commands us to give thanks to God after eating a meal: "And you shall eat and be satisfied, and bless the Lord, your God, for the good land which he has given you." (Deuteronomy 8:10) Rabbi S. R. Hirsch (1808–1888) said that ". . . even in the midst of everyday circumstances, after an ordinary meal, we are to preserve and nurture in our hearts the conviction which the miracle of the heavenly manna instilled in us in the wilderness; namely, that each and every home and soul on earth is favored by God's direct, immediate care and concern. Hence, we are to look even upon a plain piece of

Leader

The Bible indicates the obligation to say a blessing: "When you have eaten and are satisfied you shall thank the Lord your God for the good land which he has given you." (Deuteronomy 8:10)

Praised be the Lord, our God, Sovereign of all, who sustains the world with goodness and gives us the food of the earth.

Participants

We thank you, Lord our God,
for the goodly land
which you have given to our ancestors,
and for bringing us out from the land of Egypt,

bread as no less a direct gift of God than the manna." This duty is of particular significance at the seder when the celebrants remember the special value of bread eaten in freedom.

and redeeming us from the house of bondage.
We thank you for the Torah which you have taught us,
and for the life of grace and loving-kindness
which you have graciously bestowed upon us,
and for the food we eat
with which you nourish and sustain us at all times.

The Third Cup: The Cup of Redemption

The cups are filled for the third time.

Participants

The biblical text reminds us of God's redemption: "I will redeem you with an outstretched arm and with mighty acts of judgment." (Exodus 6:6)

Leader

Ba - ruh a-tah a-do-nai e-lo-hei-nu me-leh ha-o-lam bo-rei__ p'-ri ha-ga - fen.

Blessed are you, Lord our God, Ruler of the universe, creator of the fruit of the vine.

All drink the third cup of wine.

The Cup of Elijah

The door is opened for the ceremony of receiving Elijah the prophet. The cup of Elijah is filled and set in the middle of the table. After a few moments of silence, the community welcomes the expected messenger of peace.

Leader

At this moment we welcome Elijah the prophet, the messenger of final redemption and delivery from all forms of oppression.

Blessed be his presence and inspiration for all of us and humanity.

Participants

On this night of the seder
as we open the door of the house for Elijah the prophet,
we remember with reverence
those men, women and children
who perished at the hands of tyrants
more wicked than the Pharaoh
who enslaved our ancestors in Egypt.

Leader

At this moment we remember the six million Jews and their communities who were destroyed in Europe by diabolical forces that turned against all that is sacred to Jews, Christians and all other peoples who hold human life sacred and a manifestation of God.

A Participant

Moshe Flinker was still a teenager when, on the day before Passover in 1944, he and his parents and sisters were arrested by Nazi agents in Brussels and deported. Moshe and his parents perished in Auschwitz. The sisters survived the death camps and returned to Brussels after the war. Among the family's belongings they found their brother's diary. Moshe's diary, like the diary of Anne Frank, takes us into the world of those who knew with certainty that millions of Jews had already been put to death and that they themselves and the whole people had been marked for death. On January 22, 1943, Moshe learned that a family of four, which he knew well, had been taken the day before. He wrote in his diary:

The younger child was a four-year-old girl.... With all my body and soul, I wish to be with my people and share their bitter fate. When trouble befalls them so shall it befall me. I wish to be a part of my people. I do not know if I can succeed in chasing the small joys from my heart, but I shall find ways. I thought: In what condition were those people when they got into the car? Weeping? Or perhaps they steeled themselves and entered in the spirit of "In thy hand I shall trust my soul!"

...I don't know what to think, what to say, what to do. I see in the streets that the gentiles are happy and gay, and that nothing touches them. It is like being in a great hall where many people are joyful and dancing and also where there are a few people who are not happy and who are not dancing. And from time to time a few people of this latter kind are taken away, led to another room, and strangled. The happy, dancing people in the hall do not feel this at all.

Participants

At this moment we remember
all those who suffer persecution
because of their religious and spiritual beliefs.
Their witnessing in the darkness of oppression
is an inspiration for our faith communities.

Leader

We await Elijah's arrival. We ask God to inspire us by the example of all the martyrs for truth and faith, the witnesses to God in darkness and suffering. Out of the depths of affliction their testimony becomes a song of hope and faith in justice and of trust in the common bond that unites people.

Participants

All sing together "Eliyahu Hanavi," "Elijah the Prophet."

El - li - ya - hu ha - na - vi, ei - li - ya - hu ha - tish - bi,

ei - li - ya - hu, ei - li - ya - hu, ei - li - ya - hu ha - gi - la - di.

Bim - hei - ra v' - ya - mei - nu, ya - vo ei - lei - nu

im ma - shi - ah ben da - vid, im ma - shi - ah ben da - vid.

Elijah the Prophet,
Elijah the Tishbite,
Elijah the Gileadite.
In our own lifetime may he come speedily
with the Messiah, the son of David,
the Messiah, the son of David.

13. Hallel: Recital of the Psalms

The custom of reciting the hallel or praise psalms (113–118) originated in Temple days while the paschal lamb was offered, and again at night when it was eaten at the seder. The Hallel tells the story of slavery, liberation and final redemption. In this edition, we have included only one hallel psalm, Psalm 114. It is given here in the Grail translation.

Leader

When Israel came from Egypt,
Jacob's family from an alien people,
Judah became the Lord's temple,
Israel became God's kingdom.

Participants

The sea fled at the sight,
the Jordan turned back on its course,
the mountains leapt like rams
and the hills like yearling sheep.

Leader

Why was it, sea, that you fled,
that you turned back, Jordan, on your course?
Mountains, that you leapt like rams;
hills, like yearling sheep?

Participants

Tremble, O earth, before the Lord,
in the presence of the God of Jacob,
who turns the rock into a pool
and flint into a spring of water.

Songs are appropriate here. "Chad Gadyah," which follows, is traditional as is "Who Knows One?"

"Chad Gadyah" is a song intended for everyone's entertainment; it has been included in the seder since the sixteenth century. The song is seen as a symbol of God's intervention in the history of Israel. The refrain, "Chad Gadyah," means a single young goat, "one kid." This stands for Israel, redeemed by God from Egypt through Moses and Aaron who are presented as the "two *zuzim*" (two coins). Any oppression and persecution (present and future) will be ultimately redeemed in the days of the Messiah.

Who Knows One?

"Who Knows One?" is a
cumulative riddle. The main
Jewish beliefs are detailed
in the 13 stanzas of the poem,
from the central belief in one
God to the 13 attributes of
God. It is usually sung, but the
group may wish to read it,
alternating lines or verses and
making a game of its recitation.

Who knows the meaning of One?
I know One.
One is God, Lord of heaven
  and earth.

Who knows Two?
Two tables of the law,
One God of the world.

Three are the patriarchs:
Abraham, Isaac, Jacob.

Who knows Three?
Three patriarchs,
Two tables of the law,
One God of the world.

Four are the matriarchs: Sarah,
Rebecca, Leah, Rachel.

Who knows Four?
Four mothers in Israel,
Three patriarchs,
Two tables of the law,
One God of the world.

Five are the books of the
Torah: Genesis, Exodus,
Leviticus, Numbers,
Deuteronomy.

Who knows Five?
Five books of the Torah,
Four mothers in Israel,
Three patriarchs,
Two tables of the law,
One God of the world.

Six are the sections of the
Mishnah commentary to the
Bible: *Zeraim* (seeds), *Moed*
(festivals), *Nashim* (women),
Nezikin (damages), *Kodashim*
(holy things), *Toharot* (purity).

Who knows Six?
Six parts of the Mishnah,
Five books of the Torah,
Four mothers in Israel,
Three patriarchs,
Two tables of the law,
One God of the world.

Who knows Seven?
Seven days of the week,
Six parts of the Mishnah,
Five books of the Torah,
Four mothers in Israel,
Three patriarchs,
Two tables of the law,
One God of the world.

Who knows Eight?
Eight days to circumcision,
Seven days of the week,
Six parts of the Mishnah,
Five books of the Torah,
Four mothers in Israel,
Three patriarchs,
Two tables of the law,
One God of the world.

Who knows Nine?
Nine months to childbirth,
Eight days to circumcision,
Seven days of the week,
Six parts of the Mishnah,
Five books of the Torah,
Four mothers in Israel,
Three patriarchs,
Two tables of the law,
One God of the world.

Twelve are the tribes of Israel: Reuben, Simeon, Levi, Judah, Issachar, Zebulun, Dan, Naphtali, Gad, Asher, Joseph, Benjamin.

Who knows Ten?
Ten Commandments,
Nine months to childbirth,
Eight days to circumcision,
Seven days of the week,
Six parts of the Mishnah,
Five books of the Torah,
Four mothers in Israel,
Three patriarchs,
Two tables of the law,
One God of the world.

Who knows Eleven?
Eleven stars in Joseph's
    dream,
Ten Commandments,
Nine months to childbirth,
Eight days to circumcision,
Seven days of the week,
Six parts of the Mishnah,
Five books of the Torah,
Four mothers in Israel,
Three patriarchs,
Two tables of the law,
One God of the world.

Who knows Twelve?
Twelve tribes of Israel,
Eleven stars in Joseph's
    dream,
Ten Commandments,
Nine months to childbirth,
Eight days to circumcision,
Seven days of the week,
Six parts of the Mishnah,
Five books of the Torah,
Four mothers in Israel,
Three patriarchs,
Two tables of the law,
One God of the world.

Thirteen are the attributes of God. The Lord, the Lord God, compassionate, merciful, gracious, slow to anger, abundant in loving-kindness, truthful, keeping mercy unto the thousandth generation, forgiving iniquity, forgiving transgression, forgiving sin, clearing the guilty. (Exodus 34:6–7)

Who knows Thirteen?
Thirteen attributes of God,
Twelve tribes of Israel,
Eleven stars in Joseph's
    dream,
Ten Commandments,
Nine months to childbirth,
Eight days to circumcision,
Seven days of the week,
Six parts of the Mishnah,
Five books of the Torah,
Four mothers in Israel,
Three patriarchs,
Two tables of the law,
One God of the world.

14. Neertza: Conclusion of the Seder

The Cup of Hope and Freedom

The cups are filled for the fourth and final time.

All lift up their cups.

Participants

We will partake of the fourth cup of wine,
the cup of freedom.
It is a reminder of freedom —
its hopes, struggles and dreams
for so many enslaved nations and individuals.
As committed children of God,
we are called to witness this precious gift
and make it known to all peoples of the earth:
those who seek justice, those who lack any rights
and who struggle for freedom.

Leader

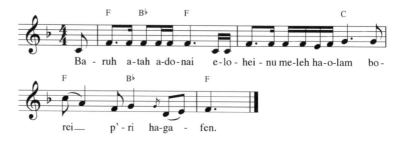

Ba - ruh a-tah a-do-nai   e-lo - hei - nu me-leh ha-o-lam   bo-

rei—   p' - ri ha-ga - fen.

Blessed are you, Lord our God, Ruler of the universe,
creator of the fruit of the vine.

All drink the fourth cup of wine.

Final Benediction: The Freedom of Jerusalem

Leader

Our Passover seder now concludes with the recital of a
poem by Rabbi Joseph Tov Elem of the eleventh century:

The rites of the Seder are now concluded
In accordance with ancient precept and custom.
With the same zeal that we have prepared for this day,
May we plan and live our daily lives.

Participants

May the Lord inspire us to nobler living
and draw us close to him.
May the battle-cry for all who seek freedom
ever ring in our ears: Next year in Jerusalem!

The shout, "Next Year in Jerusalem!" is an image of ultimate redemption, of the final Passover. Sometimes it is sung to the melody given.

Appendix

Following are two hymns that could be used at various times in the seder: e.g., just before or after the meal or at the conclusion.

God of Might (Adir Hu)

How God gave to each slave
Promised liberation,
This great word Pharaoh heard
Making proclamation:
Set them free to serve me
As a holy nation.

We, enslaved, thus were saved
Through God's might appearing.
So we pray for the day
When we shall be hearing
Freedom's call reaching all,
All life God revering.

Shalom Haverim

Sha - lom, ha-ve-rim, sha lom, ha-ve-rim, sha -
lom, sha - lom! Le - hit - ra - ot, le -
hit ra - ot, sha - lom, sha - lom!

Shalom, O my friends! Shalom, O my friends,
Shalom, shalom!
Till we meet again, till we meet again,
Shalom, shalom!

Glossary

Pronunciation Guide

ay	long **a** sound, as in gate, hay
ee	long **e** sound, as in feet, bean
oh	long **o** sound, as in goat, coat
a	short **a** sound, as in fat, cat
e	short **e** sound, as in red, bed
i	short **i** sound, as in brim, Jim
o	short **o** sound, as in hot, cot
uh	short **u** sound, as in cup
oo	pronounced as in **cool** or **book**
ea	pronounced as in **near** or **here**
ah	pronounced as in **spa** or **shah**
tzah/tzot	pronounced as in **pizza**

Notes:
—Stressed syllables are indicated by CAPS.
—In Hebrew or Yiddish, "ch" is pronounced with the letters slurred together like the word yech! *or the German word* Ich.
—Terms are Hebrew, unless otherwise noted.

afikoman
(ah–fee–KOH–mahn)

Originally from Greek, literally meaning "dessert." This refers to a special piece of matzah broken off and hidden and then returned after the meal has been eaten. This matzah is the last thing to be eaten at the seder.

beytzah
(BAY–tzah)

An egg; reminder of roasted egg offered at the Temple of Jerusalem at the Passover festival. The egg is also a symbol of the spring.

Hag Hamatzot
(Hahg | Hah–MAH–tzot)

Another name for Passover: the holiday of the unleavened bread.

Haggadah
(Hah–GAH–dah)

Meaning "the telling" of the story, and thus the ritual text used at Passover that tells the Exodus epic in prayer and proclamation.

hallel
(HAHL–el)

Praise. This is the name given to Psalms 113–118.

hametz
(HAH–mets)

Leaven, or yeast. No leavened food is to be present during Passover.

haroset
(hah–ROH–set)

Mixture of chopped apples, chopped nuts, cinnamon and wine; a visual reminder of the mortar used by the forced Hebrew laborers in Egypt; its sweetness represents freedom.

karpas
(KAHR–pahs)

A green herb (in this text parsley or celery); reminder of spring, the season of Passover; used as a sign of gratitude to God for the goodness of the earth, for our bread and food.

kiddush
(KIH–doosh)

Blessing of God recited over the wine before the evening meals of the Sabbath and festivals. The word originates from the Hebrew verb *kadesh,* meaning "to sanctify."

Mah Nishtana
(Mah | nish–TAH–nah)

"Why is this night different from all other nights?" A question posed by the youngest participants, as part of four questions traditionally asked during the seder. The answers help illustrate Passover's significance.

maror (mah–ROHR)	Bitter herb(s); reminder of bitterness and hardship of slavery. Horseradish is often used as *maror* at the seder.
manna (MAN–ah)	The bread with which God fed the Hebrew people during their years of wandering (Exodus 16).
matza (MAH–tzah)	Unleavened bread or dough without yeast that the escaping slaves took into the desert; a symbol of haste and of hope, linking exile and bondage with redemption. The plural is *matzot.*
Megillah (me–GI–lah)	Scroll, book. This is a term used for those parts of the Hebrew Bible other than the Torah and the Prophets. The plural is *Megillot.*
Mishnah (MISH–nah)	Instruction. The texts by this name were compiled about eighteen hundred years ago and deal with the practices of Jewish life.
Pesach (PAY–soch)	Passover. This is used to mean both the festival and the Passover lamb (see zeroah) that symbolizes the Lord's passing over the houses of the Hebrew slaves in Egypt, which were marked with the blood of a lamb.
seder (SAY–der)	Order. This refers to the ritual followed during the Passover meal celebration.
shalom (shah–LOHM)	Peace.
Torah (TOH–rah)	First five books of the Hebrew Scriptures, the books of Moses.
zeroah (ze–ROH–ah)	Roasted bone, a reminder of the sacrifice of the Passover lamb.
zuzim (ZOO–zim)	"two zuzim"—two coins.

About the Art

Chicago-area artist Judith Joseph created the cover, illustrations and calligraphy for *The Passover Celebration*. She uses egg tempera for her paint medium, which she mixes from pure ground pigments and egg yolk, in the style of Renaissance artists. Ms. Joseph specializes in the traditional art of the Ketubah (hand-lettered, illustrated Hebrew marriage contract).

The front cover depicts ritual objects and foods used during the seder, a feast for all senses. Mirroring the seder plate on the back cover is the full moon. This represents the Jewish lunar calendar; Passover officially begins at sundown with the presence of a full moon that evening. On page 14 an image of a Jewish woman is shown ushering in the holiday with a welcoming gesture, while she lights and blesses the candles.

Passover's epic drama emerges in the images of the illustration on pages 32–33. This illustration recalls the ten plagues recorded in Exodus. A figure in the foreground mourning the slaying of the firstborn is modeled after Egyptian statuary and was inspired by Michelangelo's Pieta.

The Haggadah imagery passes from the horrific to the holy with the composition on page 44. A small figure of Elijah is seen in the doorway, which is left open to admit him during the seder. The Star of David reminds us that, according to tradition, the appearance of Elijah will foreshadow the coming of the Messiah, a descendant of David. The empty chair brings the poignant, unseen presence of Elijah to the seder table.

Related materials available from Liturgy Training Publications

Songs for the Seder Meal, a 50-minute cassette or CD of the songs and Hebrew words used in this book, *The Passover Celebration.* Useful as a teaching tool or to accompany the singing at the seder meal.

A Blessing to Each Other: Cardinal Joseph Bernardin and Jewish-Catholic Dialogue. The Second Vatican Council set the church seeking a new relationship between Jews and Catholics. In his time as archbishop of Chicago, Cardinal Joseph Bernardin labored year after year in this dialogue. This book gathers his principal talks and columns along with outlines of central areas of concern, discussion questions and suggestions of where the dialogue must now go.

From Desolation to Hope: An Interreligious Holocaust Memorial Service, by Rabbi Leon Klenicki and Dr. Eugene Fisher. Jews and Christians have reason to remember the Holocaust, and, on some occasions, to remember it together. This may happen on the day near Passover called Yom Hashoah. This book offers all the texts and an order of service needed for such a gathering.

Thank God: Prayers of Jews and Christians Together, by Carol Francis Jegen, BVM, and Rabbi Byron L. Sherwin. A collection of prayers, stories, commentaries and brief orders of service for use at home, in small groups or in interfaith services, especially on Thanksgiving.

Teaching Christian Children about Judaism, by Deborah J. Levine. An excellent resource for religious educators and parents, this book will introduce students to the living faith and practices of Judaism. Seven complete lessons plus an audiocassette of prayers, blessings and songs in Hebrew and in English.

For more information: 1-800-933-1800.